D1498390

High-Frequency Words LEVEL C
Stories & Activities

Editorial Development: Joy Evans
Ann Rossi
Camille Liscinsky
Copy Editing: Cathy Harber
Carrie Gwynne
Art Direction: Cheryl Puckett
Cover Design: Liliana Potigian
Illustration: Dave Schimmell
Design/Production: Olivia C. Trinidad
Arynne Elfenbein

EMC 3378

Evan-Moor®
EDUCATIONAL PUBLISHERS
Helping Children Learn since 1979

Congratulations on your purchase of some of the finest teaching materials in the world.

Correlated to State Standards

For information about other Evan-Moor products, call 1-800-777-4362, fax 1-800-777-4332, or visit our Web site, www.evan-moor.com.
Entire contents © 2008 EVAN-MOOR CORP.
18 Lower Ragsdale Drive, Monterey, CA 93940-5746. Printed in USA.

Visit *teaching-standards.com* to view a correlation of this book's activities to your state's standards. This is a free service.

Contents

What's in This Book?

High-frequency words are the words that readers encounter most often in reading materials. The ability to read these high-frequency words is necessary for fluent reading. Since many high-frequency words are not phonetic, students need repeated practice to recognize the words on sight. The stories and activities in this book help students read 100 Dolch and Fry high-frequency words quickly and accurately.

15 Pretests

Use the pretests to determine which words a student needs to master. Each pretest corresponds to the high-frequency words introduced in the same-numbered unit.

15 Units

Learn New Words

On this page, students are introduced to the high-frequency words that are the unit's focus. You may wish to follow these steps to present each word:

- Point to the word, say the word, and use it in a sentence.

- Have students read the word, and then point to each letter as they spell the word aloud.

- Ask students to write the word twice, spelling the word aloud as they write it.

- At the bottom of the page, have students point to and read each word once again.

Practice New Words

Fun activities, presented in a variety of formats, give students practice in reading the unit's high-frequency words. Students may work independently or as a group.

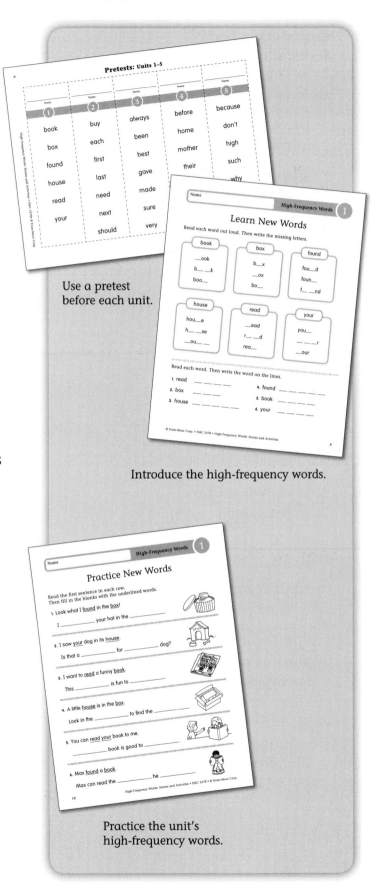

Use a pretest before each unit.

Introduce the high-frequency words.

Practice the unit's high-frequency words.

Read Naming Words

A picture dictionary introduces 3 or 4 nouns that are key to reading the story that follows. These nouns are taken from the Dolch list of 95 nouns. Students encounter the nouns individually and then in context. The unit's high-frequency words are also incorporated into the activities on the page, giving students further practice and review.

Story

The story is the unit's culminating activity. Students read the unit's high-frequency words and key story vocabulary in a meaningful context. Story vocabulary is carefully controlled, so students encounter words they can decode easily.

Word-List Slider

The slider is a wonderful tool to help students master reading the high-frequency words and key story vocabulary quickly and accurately. The slider may be used at any step in the lesson. And it is perfect for home practice!

Additional Resources

3 Cumulative Tests

Cumulative word lists follow every fifth unit. These may be used as assessment tools. Have students keep track of the number of words they read correctly. The lists also make great home practice.

Award

A reproducible certificate acknowledges the accomplishment of reading 100 high-frequency sight words.

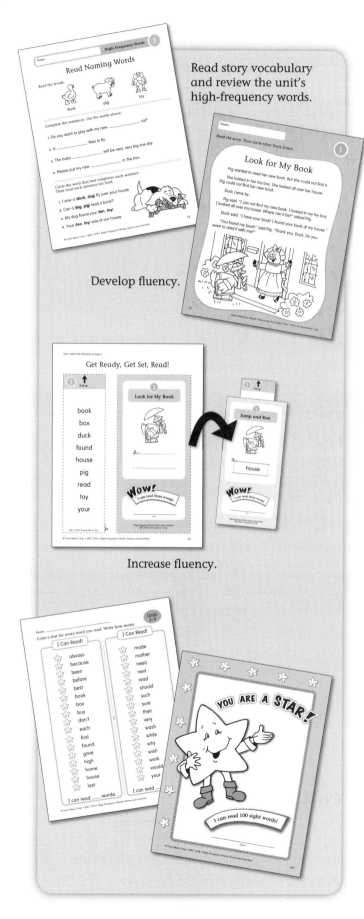

Read story vocabulary and review the unit's high-frequency words.

Develop fluency.

Increase fluency.

Pretests: Units 1–5

Name ⑤	Name ④	Name ③	Name ②	Name ①
because	before	always	buy	book
don't	home	been	each	box
high	mother	best	first	found
such	their	gave	last	house
why	wash	made	need	read
wish	while	sure	next	your
would	work	very	should	

High-Frequency Words: Stories and Activities • EMC 3378• © Evan-Moor Corp.

Pretests: Units 6–10

10	9	8	7	6
Name	Name	Name	Name	Name
ball	near	dear	both	around
cold	people	five	many	came
different	pull	friend	still	its
leave	stand	green	these	left
move	until	picture	those	name
sit	upon	write	tree	place
thing			us	right

Pretests: Units 11–15

(11) Name ___	(12) Name ___	(13) Name ___	(14) Name ___	(15) Name ___
color	call	goes	another	also
does	fast	learn	answer	even
never	father	school	end	large
off	follow	sing	mean	more
or	night	spell	morning	most
tell	sleep	study	seem	than
use		year		which

High-Frequency Words: Stories and Activities • EMC 3378• © Evan-Moor Corp.

Learn New Words

Read each word out loud. Then write the missing letters.

book

__ook

b__ __k

boo__

box

b__x

__ox

bo__

found

fou__d

foun__

f__ __nd

house

hou__e

h__ __se

__ou__ __

read

__ead

r__ __d

rea__

your

you__

__ __ __r

__our

Read each word. Then write the word on the lines.

1. read   __ __ __ __

2. box   __ __ __

3. house   __ __ __ __ __

4. found   __ __ __ __ __

5. book   __ __ __ __

6. your   __ __ __ __

Practice New Words

Read the first sentence in each row.
Then fill in the blanks with the underlined words.

1. Look what I <u>found</u> in the <u>box</u>!

I _____ your hat in the _____.

2. I saw <u>your</u> dog in its <u>house</u>.

Is that a _____ for _____ dog?

3. I want to <u>read</u> a funny <u>book</u>.

This _____ is fun to _____.

4. A little <u>house</u> is in the <u>box</u>.

Look in the _____ to find the _____.

5. You can <u>read</u> <u>your</u> book to me.

_____ book is good to _____.

6. Max <u>found</u> a <u>book</u>.

Max can read the _____ he _____.

Read Naming Words

Read the words.

duck   pig   toy

Complete the sentences. Use the words above.

1. Do you want to play with my new _____?

2. A _____ likes to fly.

3. The baby _____ will be very, very big one day.

4. Please put my new _____ in the box.

Circle the word that best completes each sentence.
Then read each sentence out loud.

1. I saw a (**duck**, **dog**) fly over your house.

2. Can a (**big**, **pig**) read a book?

3. My dog found your (**ten**, **toy**).

4. Your (**too**, **toy**) was at our house.

Name

Read the story. Then circle what Duck found.

Look for My Book

Pig wanted to read her new book. But she could not find it.

She looked in her toy box. She looked all over her house. Pig could not find her new book.

Duck came by.

Pig said, "I can not find my new book. I looked in my toy box. I looked all over my house. Where can it be?" asked Pig.

Duck said, "I have your book! I found your book at my house."

"You found my book!" said Pig. "Thank you, Duck. Do you want to read it with me?"

High-Frequency Words: Stories and Activities • EMC 3378 • © Evan-Moor Corp.

Note: Follow the directions on page 5.

Get Ready, Get Set, Read!

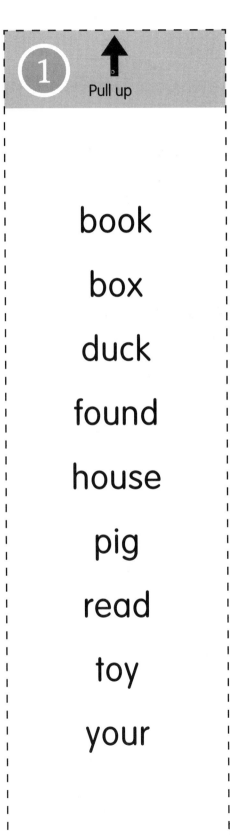

① **Pull up**

book

box

duck

found

house

pig

read

toy

your

EMC 3378 • © Evan-Moor Corp.

① **Look for My Book**

WOW!
I can read these words!

_____
Name

High-Frequency Words: Stories and Activities
EMC 3378 • © Evan-Moor Corp.

**Look for
My Book**

Learn New Words

Read each word out loud. Then write the missing letters.

buy	each	first	last
__uy	ea____	fi__st	__ast
b____	____ch	f____st	l____t
bu__	e__ch	fir____	l__s__

need	next	should
nee__	__ex__	____ould
n____d	nex__	sh____ld
__ee__	n____t	shou____

Read each word. Then write the word on the lines.

1. buy   __ __ __

5. each   __ __ __ __

2. need   __ __ __ __

6. last   __ __ __ __

3. first   __ __ __ __ __

7. should   __ __ __ __ __ __

4. next   __ __ __ __

Practice New Words

Connect the dots of the words that are the same. Use a ruler.
You will make some three-sided shapes and some four-sided shapes.
Trace the triangles in blue.

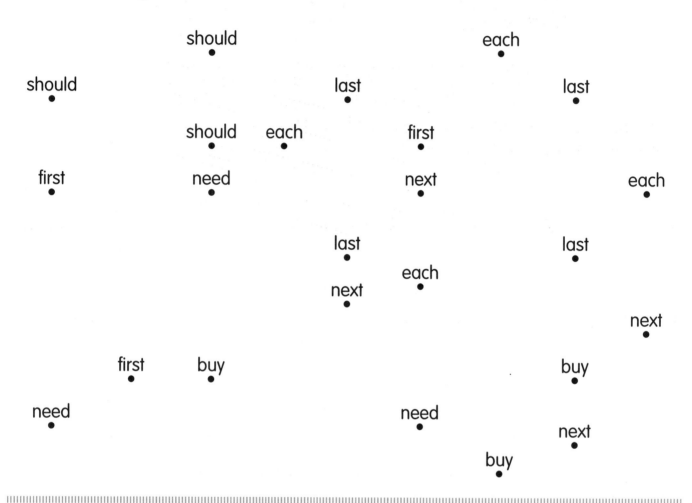

Complete the sentences. Use the words in the box.

buy   first

1. Do you want to be _____ or last to get on the bus?

2. Each of you may _____ one book at the store.

Read Naming Words

Read the words.

garden

ground

seeds

Complete the sentences. Use the words above.
Then match the words to their pictures.

1. You can make a _____.

2. First, dig into the _____.

3. Next, put in the _____.

Circle the word that best completes each sentence.
Then read each sentence out loud.

1. I will buy some (**seeds**, **sees**).

2. I need to put the seeds in the (**found**, **ground**).

3. I should keep the ducks out of my (**garden**, **ground**).

Read the story. Then circle what you like to eat.

First, Next, Last

Mike saw Lee by his garden.

Mike said, "Your garden was little when I last saw it. Now your garden is big! I want to make a garden, too. What should I do first?"

Lee said, "First, you need to buy some seeds. You can buy seeds at the garden store."

"What should I do next?" asked Mike.

Lee said, "Next, dig up the ground. Put all the seeds in the ground. Look for weeds as the seeds get big. You need to take out each weed."

Mike said, "I know what to do last. Eat the garden!"

High-Frequency Words: Stories and Activities • EMC 3378 • © Evan-Moor Corp.

Get Ready, Get Set, Read!

(2) ↑ Pull up

buy

each

first

garden

ground

last

need

next

seeds

should

EMC 3378 • © Evan-Moor Corp.

(2)

First, Next, Last

WOW!
I can read these words!

_____
Name

High-Frequency Words: Stories and Activities
EMC 3378 • © Evan-Moor Corp.

First, Next, Last

Learn New Words

Read each word out loud. Then write the missing letters.

always

al__ __ __ __

__ __ways

al__ __ __s

been

__een

b__ __n

bee__

best

bes__

b__ __ __

__ __ __t

gave

gav__

g__v__

__a__e

made

__ade

m__d__

__a__e

sure

sur__

su__e

__ure

very

__ery

ver__

v__ __y

Read each word. Then write the word on the lines.

1. gave   __ __ __ __

2. been   __ __ __ __

3. made   __ __ __ __

4. always   __ __ __ __ __ __

5. best   __ __ __ __

6. very   __ __ __ __

7. sure   __ __ __ __

Practice New Words

Use letters from the box to make words. Then read the words out loud.

1. alw__ys

2. bes__

3. __ade

4. s__re

5. ver__

6. b__en

Letter Box		
m	u	e
y	a	t

Look at the picture. Draw a line to the best ending for each sentence.

1. Pig has always made

2. Pig made sure

3. Little Bear has been

4. Little Bear thinks

5. Pig gave

6. Little Bear is sure

• the pies were big, too.

• more pies to Little Bear.

• to be Big Bear soon.

• the very best pies.

• Pig makes the best pies.

• eating pies all day.

Read Naming Words

Read the words.

birthday

cake

cow

horse

Complete the sentences. Use the words above.

1. My _____ is next week.

2. Mom always bakes me a birthday _____ .

3. We will ride a _____ .

4. We will play pin the tail on the _____ .

Circle the word that best completes each sentence.
Then read each sentence out loud.

1. My (**house**, **horse**) can jump over a very big pig.

2. I gave the (**cow**, **can**) some grass to eat.

3. The best (**cow**, **cake**) is the pink one.

4. My birthday (**sure**, **sun**) has been fun!

Name _____

Read the story. Then color the cake green, like grass.

The Very Best Birthday

"Hello, Horse. Did you know it is my birthday?" said Cow.

Horse asked, "Are you sure it is your birthday?"

Cow said, "I am sure. My birthday has always been on this day."

Horse said, "Oh, I know it is your birthday. Your birthday has always been on this day. So I made a cake for you. It is a cake made of very good grass. I know that you like to eat grass."

Horse gave the cake to Cow.

Cow said, "Thank you, Horse! Will you eat some cake with me? I know that you like to eat grass, too."

Cow gave some cake to Horse. "You made the very best cake. It is my very best birthday, too," said Cow.

High-Frequency Words: Stories and Activities • EMC 3378 • © Evan-Moor Corp.

Note: Follow the directions on page 5.

Get Ready, Get Set, Read!

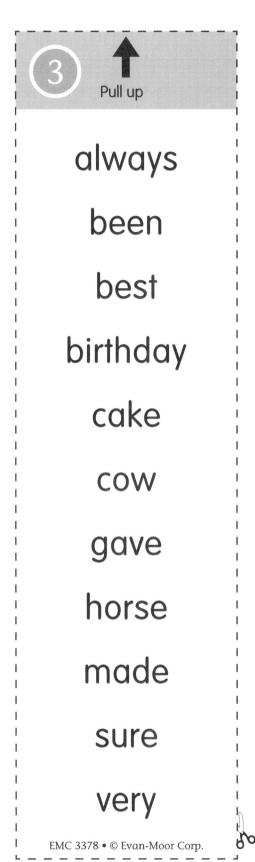

③ **Pull up**

always

been

best

birthday

cake

cow

gave

horse

made

sure

very

EMC 3378 • © Evan-Moor Corp.

③

The Very Best Birthday

WOW!
I can read these words!

_____
Name

High-Frequency Words: Stories and Activities
EMC 3378 • © Evan-Moor Corp.

The Very
Best Birthday

Learn New Words

Read each word out loud. Then write the missing letters.

before

__ __fore

be__or__

be__ __ __ __

home

h__me

hom__

__ __ __e

mother

__other

mo__ __er

m__th__ __

their

thei__

th__ __ __

__ __eir

wash

w__sh

__a__ __

wa__ __

while

__ __ile

wh__l__

wh__ __ __

work

w__ __k

__ork

wo__ __

Read each word. Then write the word on the lines.

1. their __ __ __ __ __

2. wash __ __ __ __

3. mother __ __ __ __ __ __

4. before __ __ __ __ __ __

5. work __ __ __ __

6. while __ __ __ __ __

7. home __ __ __ __

Practice New Words

Circle the two words in each box that are the same.
Then write that word on the line.

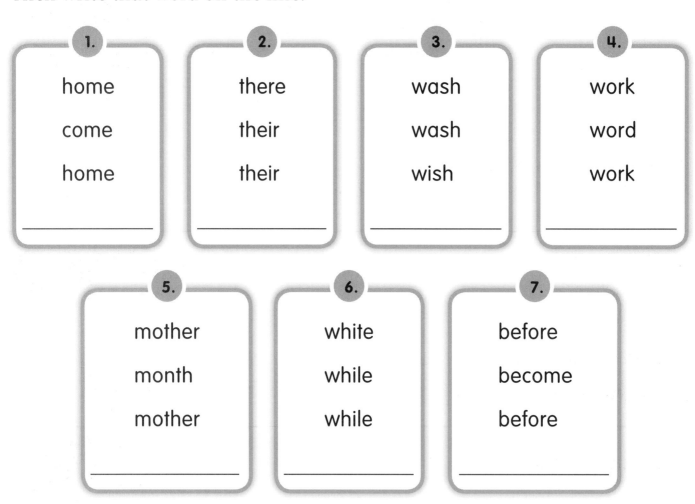

1.
home
come
home
_____

2.
there
their
their
_____

3.
wash
wash
wish
_____

4.
work
word
work
_____

5.
mother
month
mother
_____

6.
white
while
while
_____

7.
before
become
before
_____

Mark your answer.

	Yes	No
1. Do you help your mother at home?	☐	☐
2. Do you wash your hands before you eat?	☐	☐
3. Do you do work in a garden?	☐	☐
4. Do you tap your foot while you read?	☐	☐

Read Naming Words

Read the words.

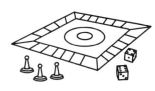

boy   car   cars   game

Complete the sentences. Use the words above.
Then match the words to their pictures.

1. We play this _____

   at home.

2. He will wash his _____

   before we go.

3. My dad had a horse when he was

   a _____.

Circle the word that best completes each sentence.
Then read each sentence out loud.

1. My mother will take us to the (**came**, **game**).

2. Their (**car**, **cars**) are parked at the house.

3. The (**boy**, **buy**) can play a game while I read.

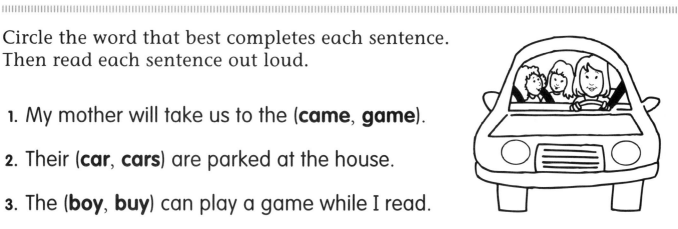

Name

Read the story. Then tell what Sam and Ben might have to do before their mother comes home.

A New Game

Sam and Ben were at home. Their mother was at work. Their dad was in the garden.

"What can we do?" asked Sam.

"We can play with our cars," said Ben.

"We played that before," said Sam. "I want to play a new game."

Ben said, "I know! We can play car wash. You get our cars while I get the hose. We need to line up our cars before we play."

The cars were very wet in the car wash. Each boy was wet, too.

While Sam and Ben played, Dad came by. He said, "Your mother will be home from work soon. I was going to ask you to wash up. But it looks like the car wash is a boy wash, too!"

High-Frequency Words: Stories and Activities • EMC 3378 • © Evan-Moor Corp.

Note: Follow the directions on page 5.

Get Ready, Get Set, Read!

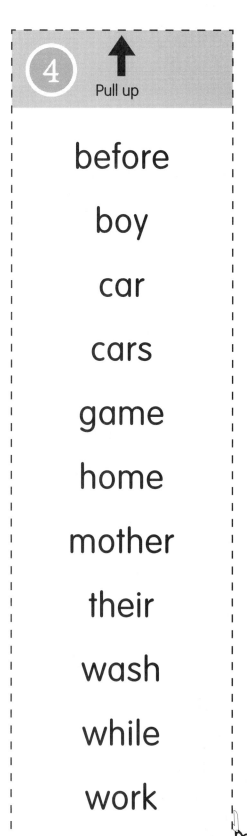

④ Pull up

before

boy

car

cars

game

home

mother

their

wash

while

work

EMC 3378 • © Evan-Moor Corp.

④

A New Game

WOW!
I can read these words!

_____
Name

High-Frequency Words: Stories and Activities
EMC 3378 • © Evan-Moor Corp.

A New Game

High-Frequency Words: Stories and Activities • EMC 3378 • © Evan-Moor Corp.

Learn New Words

Read each word out loud. Then write the missing letters.

because
__ __cause
bec__ __se
becau__ __

don't
do__'__
__ __n't
__o__'__

high
__igh
h__ __ __
hig__

such
suc__
s__c__
__uch

why
__hy
w__y
wh__

wish
wi__ __
__ish
w__ __ __

would
wou__d
__ould
w__ __ld

Read each word. Then write the word on the lines.

1. such   __ __ __ __

2. don't   __ __ __'__

3. wish   __ __ __ __

4. because __ __ __ __ __ __ __

5. why   __ __ __

6. high   __ __ __ __

7. would __ __ __ __ __

Practice New Words

Use letters from the box to make words. Then read the words out loud.

1. __ish   3. don'__   5. wh__

2. hi__h   4. wou__d   6. su__h

Letter Box		
t	c	w
l	g	y

Look at the picture. Draw a line to the best ending for each sentence.

1. "I wish I could   • because you would go up too high," said Mom.

2. "I don't think   • go on that ride," said Bart.

3. "Why would I   • fun to go up high," said Bart.

4. "You would not like it   • not like that ride?" asked Bart.

5. "But it looks like such   • you would like that ride," said Mom.

6. "Why don't you go on   • this other ride?" asked Mom.

Read Naming Words

Read the words.

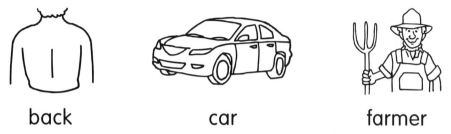

back   car   farmer

Complete the sentences. Use the words above.

1. The _____ will buy a cow and some pigs.

2. A bug bit me on my _____.

3. That is such a little _____ to ride in!

Circle the word that best completes each sentence.
Then read each sentence out loud.

1. Would you like a ride in our new (**cake**, **car**)?

2. Don't you see the spot on my (**black**, **back**)?

3. I wish the (**farmer**, **farm**) would give me a pig.

Name _____

Read the story. Then draw a face to show how Pig feels at the end.
Use a sheet of paper.

Pig Has a Wish

One day, Pig said, "I wish I could fly."

"Pigs don't fly," said Duck. "Why do you have such an odd wish?"

Pig said, "I want to fly because it would be such fun!"

Duck said, "It is fun to fly. Get on my back. I will take you for a ride."

Pig sat on Duck's back. Soon, they were up very high.

Pig looked down at the ground. Pig saw a farmer. The farmer was as little as a doll. Pig saw a car. The car was as little as a toy. That was because Pig was up so high.

"I would like to go down now!" said Pig.

"Why do you want to go down?" asked Duck.

"I don't like to be up high!" said Pig. "Now I know why pigs don't fly!"

High-Frequency Words: Stories and Activities • EMC 3378 • © Evan-Moor Corp.

Get Ready, Get Set, Read!

Pig Has
a Wish

High-Frequency Words: Stories and Activities • EMC 3378 • © Evan-Moor Corp.

Name _____

Color a star for every word you read. Write how many.

I Can Read!

 always
 because
 been
 before
 best
 book
 box
 buy
 don't
 each
 first
 found
 gave
 high
 home
 house
 last

I can read ____ words.

fold

I Can Read!

 made
 mother
 need
 next
 read
 should
 such
 sure
 their
 very
 wash
 while
 why
 wish
 work
 would
 your

I can read ____ words.

Learn New Words

Read each word out loud. Then write the missing letters.

came	its	left	name
__ame	i__ __	__e__t	n__ __e
cam__	it__	lef__	__ __me
c__ __e	__t__	le__ __	__ame

around	place	right
ar__ __nd	__ __ace	__ __ght
arou__ __	pl__ce	r__ __ __t
a__ __ __ __ __	plac__	righ__

Read each word. Then write the word on the lines.

1. left   __ __ __ __

2. place   __ __ __ __ __

3. its   __ __ __

4. around __ __ __ __ __ __

5. name   __ __ __ __

6. came   __ __ __ __

7. right   __ __ __ __ __

Practice New Words

Circle the two words in each box that are the same.
Then write that word on the line.

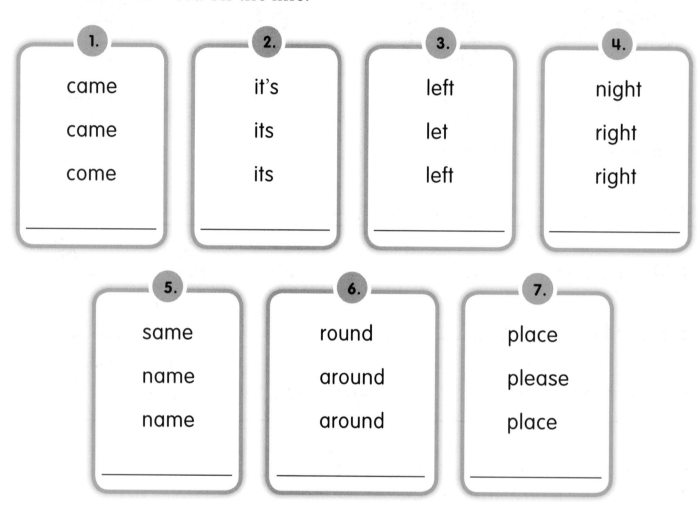

1.
came
came
come
_____

2.
it's
its
its
_____

3.
left
let
left
_____

4.
night
right
right
_____

5.
same
name
name
_____

6.
round
around
around
_____

7.
place
please
place
_____

Mark your answer.

	Yes	No
1. Do you know your left from your right?	☐	☐
2. Can you name the place where you live?	☐	☐
3. Do you and your mother have the same name?	☐	☐
4. Can a cow say its name?	☐	☐

Read Naming Words

Read the words.

eye   girl   ring   street

Complete the sentences. Use the words above.

1. That _____ lives on my street.

2. There is a bug in my left _____!

3. I found a ball on my _____.

4. My cat has a _____ around its tail and its eye.

Circle the word that best completes each sentence.
Then read each sentence out loud.

1. I made a (**ride**, **ring**) around my name.

2. What is the name of that (**give**, **girl**)?

3. My right (**every**, **eye**) is blue and my left (**eye**, **ever**) is brown.

4. Turn left to get to my (**street**, **sweet**).

Read the story. Then color the rings around the dog's eyes.

A Place for a Dog

Anna saw a dog in the street. She said, "Come here! The street is not a good place for a dog."

The dog came to Anna. The dog had a black ring around its left eye. It had a white ring around its right eye.

Anna saw a girl come out of a house. The girl looked to her right, and she looked to her left. Then she came over to Anna and the dog.

"Hi! My name is Jan," said the girl. "That is my dog Ringo. I do not want Ringo to run in the street."

Anna told the girl her name. Then Anna said, "I am going to the park. Do you and Ringo want to play with me?"

"Sure! The park would be a good place for a dog," said Jan.

"Woof!" said Ringo.

Note: Follow the directions on page 5.

Get Ready, Get Set, Read!

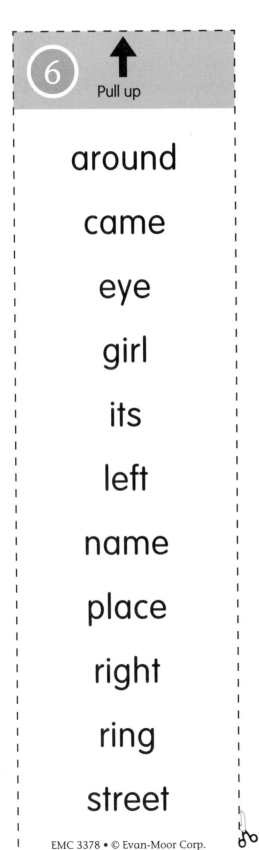

(6) ↑ Pull up

around

came

eye

girl

its

left

name

place

right

ring

street

(6)

A Place for a Dog

WOW!
I can read these words!

Name

A Place for a Dog

Learn New Words

Read each word out loud. Then write the missing letters.

both

bo__ __

b__th

__oth

many

__any

man__

ma__ __

still

st__ __ __

__ __ill

s__i__ __

these

th__ __e

__ __ese

th__s__

those

__ __ose

th__se

tho__ __

tree

__ree

t__ee

tr__ __

us

__s

u__

Read each word. Then write the word on the lines.

1. tree _____ _____ _____ _____

2. many _____ _____ _____ _____

3. still _____ _____ _____ _____ _____

4. those _____ _____ _____ _____ _____

5. these _____ _____ _____ _____ _____

6. both _____ _____ _____ _____

7. us _____ _____

Practice New Words

Connect the dots of the words that are the same. Use a ruler.
You will make some three-sided shapes and some four-sided shapes.
Trace the four-sided shapes in green.

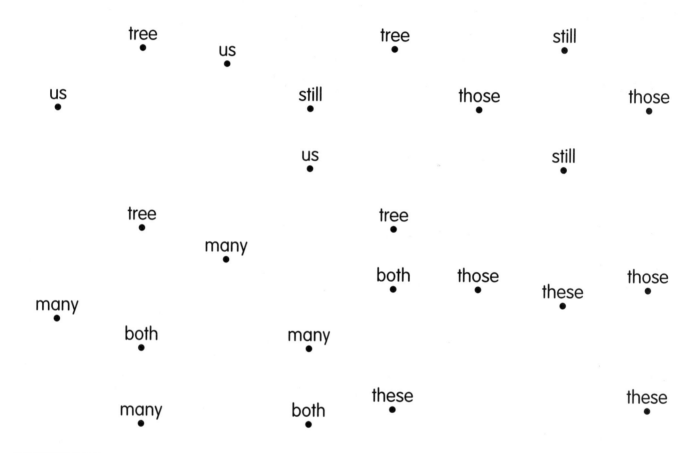

tree us   tree   still

us   still   those   those

us   still

tree   tree

many   both   those   those
                    these

many   both   many

both   these   these

Complete the sentences. Use the words in the box.

| many   still   these |

1. Can you _____ play with me?

2. How _____ of _____ books do you want?

Read Naming Words

Read the words.

apples   rabbit   rabbits   squirrel

Complete the sentences. Use the words above.
Then match the words to their pictures.

1. The brown _____

   ran up the tree.

2. There are many _____

   on the tree.

3. The little _____

   hops by both of us.

Circle the word that best completes each sentence.
Then read each sentence out loud.

1. I will give those (**apes**, **apples**) to these horses.

2. Can both of you jump like (**duck**, **rabbits**)?

Read the story. Then color the apples you would eat.

Those Apples

Ricky Rabbit and Rocky Rabbit came to a tree. They saw apples on the ground. Ricky said, "Many of these apples look good to eat."

Rocky said, "I don't want these apples that are on the ground. Look! Many apples are still at the top of the tree. I want those apples. Let us jump and get them!"

Both rabbits jumped as high as they could. They still could not get the apples.

Squirrel came by. Rocky asked, "Can you help us? We want those apples at the top of the tree."

"Sure," said Squirrel. "I will get those apples for you."

Many apples came down from the tree.

"Thanks, Squirrel!" said both of the rabbits.

High-Frequency Words: Stories and Activities • EMC 3378 • © Evan-Moor Corp.

Note: Follow the directions on page 5.

Get Ready, Get Set, Read!

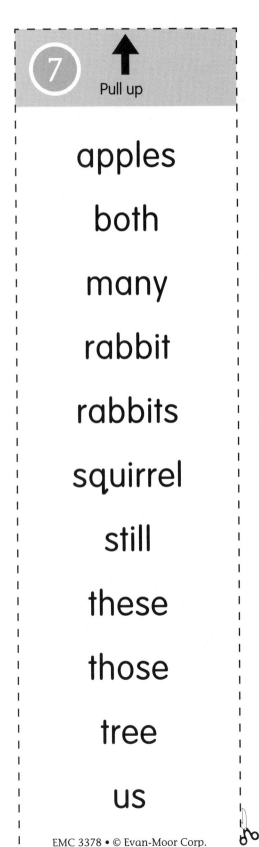

(7) ↑ Pull up

apples

both

many

rabbit

rabbits

squirrel

still

these

those

tree

us

EMC 3378 • © Evan-Moor Corp.

7

Those Apples

WOW!
I can read these words!

_____
Name

High-Frequency Words: Stories and Activities
EMC 3378 • © Evan-Moor Corp.

Those Apples

 High-Frequency Words: Stories and Activities • EMC 3378 • © Evan-Moor Corp.

Learn New Words

Read each word out loud. Then write the missing letter or letters.

dear

__ear

d__ __ __

d__ __r

five

fiv__

__i__e

f__ __e

friend

fri__ __ __

fr__end

__ __iend

green

__ __een

gr__ __n

gree__

picture

pic__ __ __ __

__ic__ __ __e

__ __ __ture

write

__rite

wr__ __e

wr__t__

‖‖

Read each word. Then write the word on the lines.

1. five   __ __ __ __

2. dear   __ __ __ __

3. friend   __ __ __ __ __ __

4. picture __ __ __ __ __ __ __

5. green   __ __ __ __ __

6. write   __ __ __ __ __

Practice New Words

Read the first sentence in each row.
Then fill in the blanks with the underlined words.

1. Do you <u>write</u> to a <u>friend</u>?

   My _____ Emma and I _____ every week.

2. These <u>five</u> <u>green</u> bugs don't bite.

   The _____ bugs are on the _____ grass.

3. I have a <u>picture</u> of my <u>dear</u> dog.

   My _____ dog is in the _____.

4. My <u>friend</u> will take my <u>picture</u>.

   My _____ Cody and I will be in the _____.

5. I will <u>write</u> some words in <u>green</u>, orange, and red.

   Can you _____ "Hello" in _____?

6. Homer has <u>five</u> <u>dear</u> cats.

   The _____ cats are _____ to Homer.

High-Frequency Words: Stories and Activities • EMC 3378 • © Evan-Moor Corp.

Read Naming Words

Read the words.

farm

fish

letter

sheep

Complete the sentences. Use the words above.
Then match the words to their pictures.

1. We have some new _____

   at our _____.

2. I will write a _____

   to my dear friend.

3. Those are funny _____!

Circle the word that best completes each sentence.

1. We have five black (**sleep**, **sheep**) on our farm.

2. I have a (**let**, **letter**) from my dear friend.

3. Can a (**find**, **fish**) write with its fin?

8

Read the story. Draw what is missing. Then color the fish.

Write a Letter, Get a Letter

I want to write a letter to my friend Ann. She lives on a farm. This is what I will write.

Dear Ann,

I have five new fish.

They are orange and green.

Here is a picture of them.

Please write soon.

Your friend,

Rosa

Here is a letter that came from Ann.

Dear Rosa,

I like your five new fish.
We have five new sheep
at the farm.
They like to eat green grass.
Can you come see the sheep?
We can make a picture of them!

Your friend,

ann

High-Frequency Words: Stories and Activities • EMC 3378 • © Evan-Moor Corp.

Note: Follow the directions on page 5.

Get Ready, Get Set, Read!

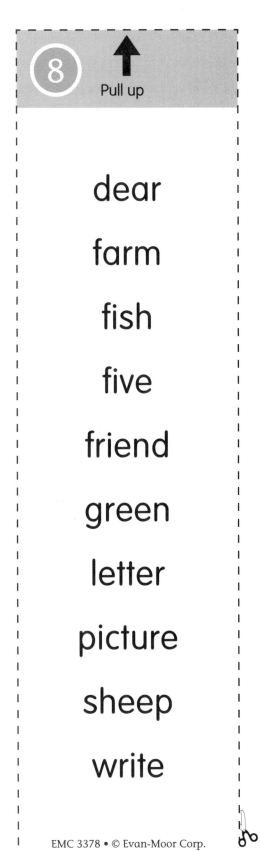

8 ↑ Pull up

dear

farm

fish

five

friend

green

letter

picture

sheep

write

8

**Write a Letter,
Get a Letter**

WOW!
I can read these words!

_____
Name

High-Frequency Words: Stories and Activities
EMC 3378 • © Evan-Moor Corp.

Dear Ann,
I have five new fish.
They are orange and green.
Here is a picture of them.

Please write soon,
Your friend,

Rosa

Write a Letter,
Get a Letter

Learn New Words

Read each word out loud. Then write the missing letters.

near	people	pull
__ear	__ __ __ple	pu__ __
n__ __ __	p__o__le	p__ll
n__ __r	p__ __ple	p__ __ __ __

stand	until	upon
__ __and	un__ __ __	__ __on
st__ __ __	__ __til	up__ __
s__an__	__nti__	__pon

Read each word. Then write the word on the lines.

1. near   __ __ __ __

2. people   __ __ __ __ __ __

3. pull   __ __ __ __

4. stand   __ __ __ __ __

5. until   __ __ __ __ __

6. upon   __ __ __ __

Practice New Words

Circle the two words in each box that are the same.
Then write that word on the line.

1.

next

near

near

_____

2.

people

purple

people

_____

3.

pull

pull

put

_____

4.

upon

open

upon

_____

5.

said

stand

stand

_____

6.

until

under

until

_____

Mark your answer.

	Yes	No
1. Can you stand upon a box?	☐	☐
2. Do you live near a farm?	☐	☐
3. Can you pull a car with people in it?	☐	☐
4. Is it a week until your birthday?	☐	☐

Read Naming Words

Read the words.

bird

nest

robin

robins

Complete the sentences. Use the words above.
Then match the words to their pictures.

1. A big black _____

   is in the tree.

2. The eggs in the _____

   are blue.

3. I see a _____

   with a worm.

Circle the word that best completes each sentence.
Then read each sentence out loud.

1. The people saw a (**robin**, **round**) sit upon its nest.

2. I saw a (**bed**, **bird**) pull a worm out of the grass.

3. Kate saw robins work to make a (**nest**, **next**).

Name

Read the story. Then color the robin.

What Is a Robin?

What bird is in the picture? The bird is a robin. A robin has a gray back. Its underpart is red. People see the red when robins run upon the ground.

Robins may live near people. They may make a nest with grass. The nest may be in a tree. The tree may be near a house.

Many people like to watch robins eat. Robins run to look for food. They run and then they stand still until they see a worm. They pull the worm out of the ground. Then robins run and stop again. They stand still until they see the next worm. Then they pull out that one.

When you go out, look for a robin. The bird may be running upon the ground. See if the bird will find a worm to eat.

 High-Frequency Words: Stories and Activities • EMC 3378 • © Evan-Moor Corp.

Note: Follow the directions on page 5.

Get Ready, Get Set, Read!

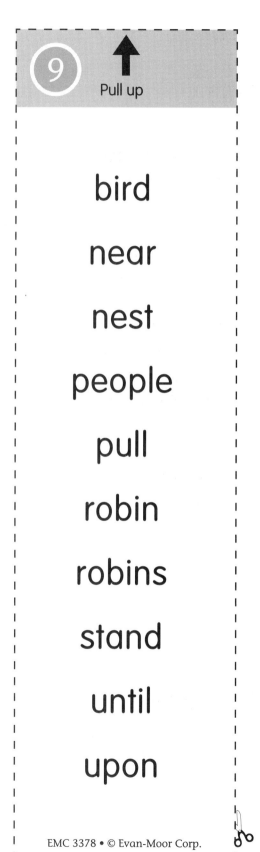

⑨ **Pull up** ↑

bird

near

nest

people

pull

robin

robins

stand

until

upon

⑨

What Is a Robin?

WOW! I can read these words!

_____
Name

What Is a Robin?

High-Frequency Words: Stories and Activities • EMC 3378 • © Evan-Moor Corp.

Learn New Words

Read each word out loud. Then write the missing letters.

ball

_all

b_ _ _

bal_

cold

c_ _ _

_old

c_l_

leave

eav

l_ _ve

lea_ _

move

m_ve

mo_ _

_ov_

sit

_it

s_ _

s_t

thing

th_ _ _

_ _ing

t_ing

different

differ_ _ _

_ _ _ferent

dif_ _ _ent

Read each word. Then write the word on the lines.

1. move   __ __ __ __

2. cold   __ __ __ __

3. ball   __ __ __ __

4. different   __ __ __ __ __ __ __ __ __

5. sit   __ __ __

6. thing   __ __ __ __ __

7. leave   __ __ __ __ __

Practice New Words

Read the first sentence in each row.
Then fill in the blanks with the underlined words.

1. You had a <u>different</u> <u>ball</u> last week.

How was the _____ _____?

2. I like to <u>sit</u> in a <u>cold</u> pool when it is hot.

Is the pool too _____ to _____ in?

3. We must <u>move</u> this big <u>thing</u>.

Where must you _____ this _____?

4. Please <u>leave</u> the <u>ball</u> at home.

I will _____ the _____ there.

5. I want to <u>move</u> to a <u>different</u> house.

What is _____ about this _____?

6. Where should I <u>sit</u> when you <u>leave</u>?

When I _____, you can _____ here.

Read Naming Words

Read the words.

baby

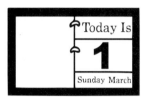

chicken

day

egg

Complete the sentences. Use the words above.
Then match the words to their pictures.

1. On what _____

   is your birthday?

2. Can you see the chicken come

   out of its _____?

3. Move the _____

   before you sit down!

Circle the word that best completes each sentence.
Then read each sentence out loud.

1. I was cold all (**day**, **egg**) long.

2. The egg of a (**chicken**, **ball**) is different from the egg of a robin.

3. I will give this pink thing to the (**big**, **baby**).

Read the story. About how many days does a baby chick stay in its egg?

A Different Day

One day, Chicken found an odd thing in her nest. It was round like a ball, but it was not a ball. It was different. Chicken said, "I think this thing is my first egg. I will sit on my egg all day so it will not get cold. I will not leave my egg."

Chicken would move her egg over a little bit every day. Then she would sit on a different side of the egg. She did not leave her egg. She did not let her egg get cold.

After three weeks, Chicken saw her egg move. She saw it move again. Then a baby chicken came out of the egg.

Chicken said, "You are my baby. You are different from me. You are little and yellow. But you are still my baby."

High-Frequency Words: Stories and Activities • EMC 3378 • © Evan-Moor Corp.

Note: Follow the directions on page 5.

Get Ready, Get Set, Read!

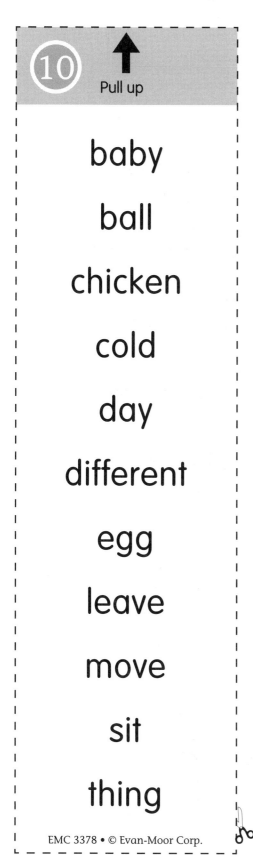

⑩ ↑
Pull up

baby

ball

chicken

cold

day

different

egg

leave

move

sit

thing

EMC 3378 • © Evan-Moor Corp.

⑩

A Different Day

✂ — — — — — — —

- - - - - - - - - -

WOW!
I can read these words!

_____
Name

High-Frequency Words: Stories and Activities
EMC 3378 • © Evan-Moor Corp.

A Different Day

Name _____

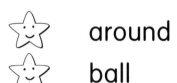

Color a star for every word you read. Write how many.

I Can Read!

☆ around
☆ ball
☆ both
☆ came
☆ cold
☆ dear
☆ different
☆ five
☆ friend
☆ green
☆ its
☆ leave
☆ left
☆ many
☆ move
☆ name
☆ near

I can read ____ words.

fold

I Can Read!

☆ people
☆ picture
☆ place
☆ pull
☆ right
☆ sit
☆ stand
☆ still
☆ these
☆ thing
☆ those
☆ tree
☆ until
☆ upon
☆ us
☆ write

I can read ____ words.

72

Learn New Words

Read each word out loud. Then write the missing letters.

color	does	never	off
co___ ___ ___	___oes	nev___ ___	___ff
___ ___lor	d___e___	___ever	of___
co___or	doe___	n___ ___ ___r	o___ ___

or	tell	use
o___	t___ ___ ___	us___
___r	te___ ___	u___e
	___ell	___se

Read each word. Then write the word on the lines.

1. color   ___ ___ ___ ___ ___

2. tell   ___ ___ ___ ___

3. never   ___ ___ ___ ___ ___

4. use   ___ ___ ___

5. or   ___ ___

6. does   ___ ___ ___ ___

7. off   ___ ___ ___

Practice New Words

Connect the dots of the words that are the same. Use a ruler.
You will make some three-sided shapes and some four-sided shapes.
Trace the triangles in red.

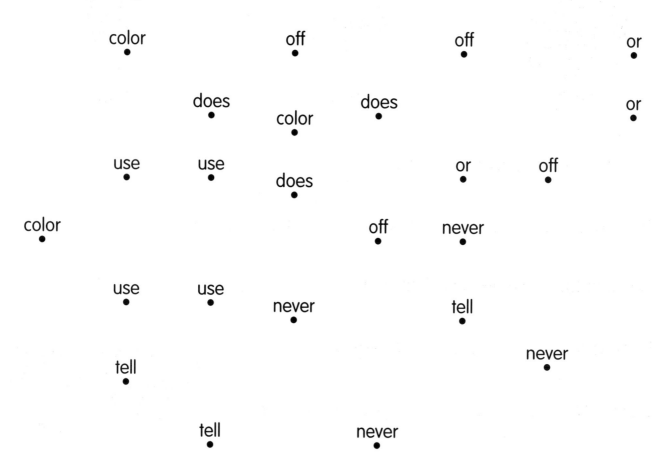

Complete the sentences. Use the words in the box.

> use   off   does   never

1. I can _____ get the top _____ this jar.

2. _____ your mother _____ her car for work?

   High-Frequency Words: Stories and Activities • EMC 3378 • © Evan-Moor Corp.

Read Naming Words

Read the words.

party

sister

watch

Complete the sentences. Use the words above.

1. My big _____ never lets me use her toys.

2. What color cake will you have at your _____?

3. I use my _____ every day.

4. Does your _____ play with you?

Circle the word that best completes each sentence.
Then read each sentence out loud.

1. Dad takes off his (**wash**, **watch**) when he gets home.

2. Do you want a (**party**, **watch**) at home or at the park?

3. Tell me when you will have a birthday (**part**, **party**).

4. Does your (**summer**, **sister**) use your things?

Read the story. Make an **X** to show where Rob found the watch.

A Watch Comes Off

Jess said, "My sister let me use her watch. I put it on for a party. Now I don't know where the watch is!"

Rob asked, "Does your sister know you don't have the watch?"

Jess said, "She does not know. And I don't want to tell her. I have to find her watch. She will never let me use her things again!"

Rob asked, "Tell me, did you take off the watch at the party?"

"I never did," said Jess. "But the watch did come off when we had cake. I put the watch on again. I have cake left over."

Rob looked at the cake. He asked, "What color is the watch? Is the watch a dark brown color? I think I have found it. Good thing you did not eat all of your cake, or you would tell time!"

High-Frequency Words: Stories and Activities • EMC 3378 • © Evan-Moor Corp.

Note: Follow the directions on page 5.

Get Ready, Get Set, Read!

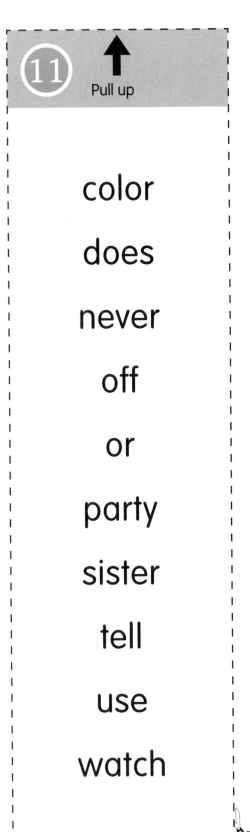

(11) ↑ Pull up

color

does

never

off

or

party

sister

tell

use

watch

(11)

A Watch Comes Off

WOW!
I can read these words!

Name

A Watch
Comes Off

Learn New Words

Read each word out loud. Then write the missing letters.

call

c__ __ __

__all

cal__

fast

f__ __t

fas__

__as__

father

fath__ __

__ __ther

fa__ __ __ __

follow

fol__ __ __

f__ll__w

__ __ __low

night

n__ __ __t

__ight

nigh__

sleep

__ __eep

sl__ __p

s__ee__

Read each word. Then write the word on the lines.

1. fast   __ __ __ __

2. sleep   __ __ __ __ __

3. father   __ __ __ __ __ __

4. follow   __ __ __ __ __ __

5. night   __ __ __ __ __

6. call   __ __ __ __

Practice New Words

Circle the two words in each box that are the same.
Then write that word on the line.

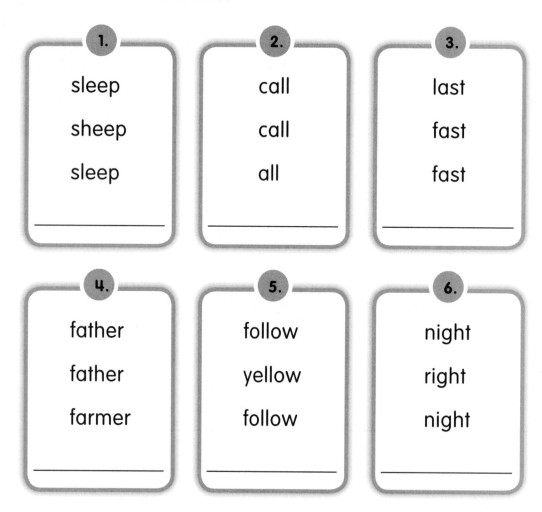

1.

sleep

sheep

sleep

_____

2.

call

call

all

_____

3.

last

fast

fast

_____

4.

father

father

farmer

_____

5.

follow

yellow

follow

_____

6.

night

right

night

_____

Mark your answer.

	Yes	No
1. Do you sleep at night?	☐	☐
2. Can your father run fast?	☐	☐
3. Does **three** follow **four**?	☐	☐
4. Can you call a bug?	☐	☐

High-Frequency Words: Stories and Activities • EMC 3378 • © Evan-Moor Corp.

Read Naming Words

Read the words.

bed

fire

time

Complete the sentences. Use the words above.

1. You should run fast from a _____.

2. I read in _____ at night before I go to sleep.

3. At what _____ do you get up?

Circle the word that best completes each sentence.
Then read each sentence out loud.

1. I would call for help if I saw a (**first**, **fire**).

2. My (**bed**, **red**) looks like a car.

3. My sister said it is (**time**, **fire**) for me to come home.

4. The teacher said to follow her if there is a (**fire**, **five**).

Read the story. Then talk about what to do when there is a fire.

Fire in the Night

It was time for bed, so Kate went to sleep. In the still of the night, her father had a call. It was a call for help.

Father jumped out of bed fast! It was not time for him to sleep. There was a fire at a house. Father had to leave right away.

Father dashed to the fire. He saw the house and went in. He said to the people, "I will help you. You must follow me. We must get out of the house as fast as we can!"

The people had to follow Father. He got them out of the house.

Father came home after the fire was out. He went right to sleep. He would be ready for the next call for help.

High-Frequency Words: Stories and Activities • EMC 3378 • © Evan-Moor Corp.

Note: Follow the directions on page 5.

Get Ready, Get Set, Read!

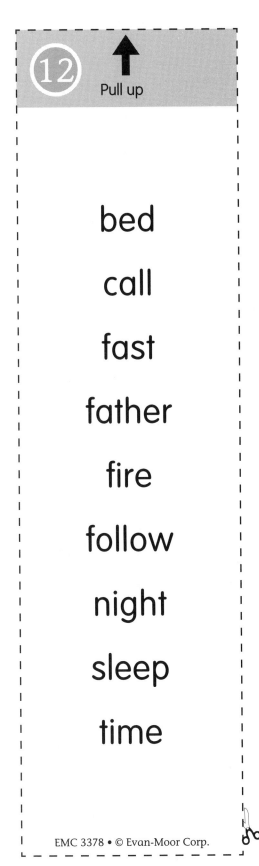

bed

call

fast

father

fire

follow

night

sleep

time

EMC 3378 • © Evan-Moor Corp.

Fire in
the Night

High-Frequency Words: Stories and Activities • EMC 3378 • © Evan-Moor Corp.

Learn New Words

Read each word out loud. Then write the missing letters.

goes
g__es
__ __es
go__ __

learn
__e__rn
l__ __ __n
__ea__ __

school
sch__ __l
__ __ __ool
sc__oo__

sing
__ing
s__ __ __
s__ __g

spell
__ __ell
sp__ __ __
sp__l__

study
st__ __y
__ __udy
stud__

year
y__ __ __
yea__
__ear

Read each word. Then write the word on the lines.

1. sing   __ __ __ __

2. goes   __ __ __ __

3. learn   __ __ __ __ __

4. school   __ __ __ __ __ __

5. year   __ __ __ __

6. study   __ __ __ __ __

7. spell   __ __ __ __ __

Practice New Words

Use letters from the box to make words. Then read the words out loud.

1. g__es   3. si__g   5. le__rn

2. sc__ool   4. spe__l   6. stud__

Letter Box		
n	h	l
y	a	o

Look at the picture. Draw a line to the best ending for each sentence.

1. One pig   • to spell words.

2. One horse can   • not for people.

3. Two chickens learn   • goes to sleep.

4. Three chickens   • goes in the school.

5. One sheep   • stand and sing.

6. The school is   • study their books.

Read Naming Words

Read the words.

boy

children

song

Complete the sentences. Use the words above.

1. We will learn to sing a _____ this year.

2. The _____ study their books.

3. That _____ goes to my school.

4. Can the _____ spell all the words?

Circle the word that best completes each sentence.
Then read each sentence out loud.

1. Did that (**song**, **boy**) go to our school last year?

2. The (**child**, **children**) learn to spell words every day.

3. Would you like to sing a (**song**, **spring**)?

4. One of their children is a (**boy**, **bug**).

Read the story. Tell how you think Kim feels before and after the song.
You can sing the song to the tune of "A Hunting We Will Go."

The Song Goes Like This

A new boy came to school this year. His name was Kim. The children did not know him. The boy did not know the children.

Miss Winters said to Kim, "The children like to sing. They made up a song to sing for you. It goes like this:"

This is our school.
We think that it is cool.
We study and spell.
We learn to work well.
We want you at our school.

Don't you fear.
You will have a good year.
You can study and spell.
You can learn to work well.
We want you at our school.

Kim said, "I like the song. I think I will like this school, too."

High-Frequency Words: Stories and Activities • EMC 3378 • © Evan-Moor Corp.

Note: Follow the directions on page 5.

Get Ready, Get Set, Read!

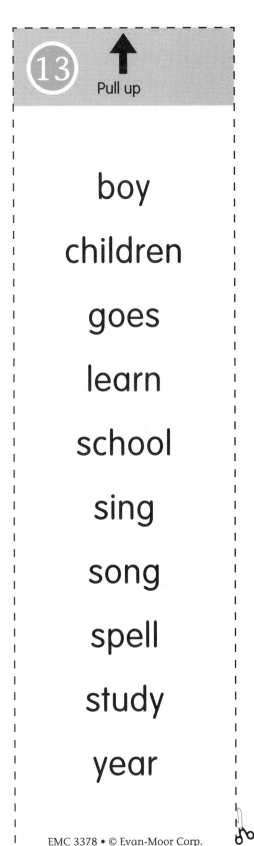

(13) ↑
Pull up

boy

children

goes

learn

school

sing

song

spell

study

year

EMC 3378 • © Evan-Moor Corp.

13
The Song Goes Like This

WOW!
I can read these words!

_____
Name

High-Frequency Words: Stories and Activities
EMC 3378 • © Evan-Moor Corp.

The Song
Goes Like This

High-Frequency Words: Stories and Activities • EMC 3378 • © Evan-Moor Corp.

Learn New Words

Read each word out loud. Then write the missing letters.

another

an__ __ __ __ __

ano__ __er

an__th__ __

answer

__ __swer

ans__er

ans__ __ __

end

e__ __

en__

e__d

mean

m__ __n

__ean

mea__

morning

morn__ __ __

m__ __nin__

__or__in__

seem

__eem

s__ __m

see__

Read each word. Then write the word on the lines.

1. end   __ __ __

2. seem   __ __ __ __

3. another   __ __ __ __ __ __ __

4. answer   __ __ __ __ __ __

5. morning   __ __ __ __ __ __ __

6. mean   __ __ __ __

Practice New Words

Circle the two words in each box that are the same.
Then write that word on the line.

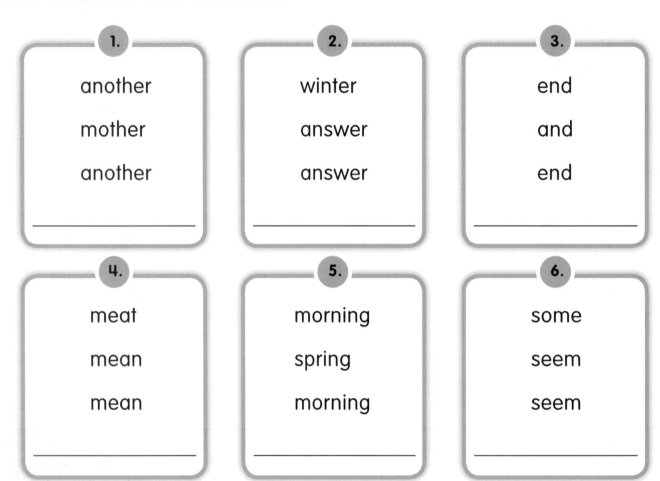

1.

another

mother

another

_____

2.

winter

answer

answer

_____

3.

end

and

end

_____

4.

meat

mean

mean

_____

5.

morning

spring

morning

_____

6.

some

seem

seem

_____

Mark your answer.

	Yes	No
1. Does **another** mean "one more"?	☐	☐
2. Is the morning the end of the day?	☐	☐
3. Does a duck seem like a chicken?	☐	☐
4. Do you like to answer these things?	☐	☐

Read Naming Words

Read the words.

head

money

paper

Complete the sentences. Use the words above.
Then match the words to their pictures.

1. Eva will write her answer on

   the _____.

2. The dog has a bug on its

   _____.

3. I gave Jon some _____

   this morning.

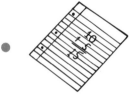

Circle the word that best completes each sentence.
Then read each sentence out loud.

1. Can I write the answer on another (**people**, **paper**)?

2. I seem to have no more (**money**, **mean**).

3. You use your (**had**, **head**) to study.

Read the story. Then tell a riddle that you know.

Ask and Answer

One morning, Mom gave Jack and Jill some money. They went to a store. They looked at books all morning.

Jill said, "This book sure does seem funny. I will ask you some things. You give the answer. Ready?"

When can you use paper to buy a toy?

Jack said, "I know! When the paper is money."

Jill said, "Right! Here is another one."

What has no end?

Jill said, "You don't seem to know the answer. A ring has no end."

"I don't get it," said Jack. "What do you mean?"

Jill said, "A ring is round, so it has no end. Here is another one."

What can you stand on and think with?

"Your head! I mean, my head!" said Jack. "We should buy this book."

 High-Frequency Words: Stories and Activities • EMC 3378 • © Evan-Moor Corp.

Get Ready, Get Set, Read!

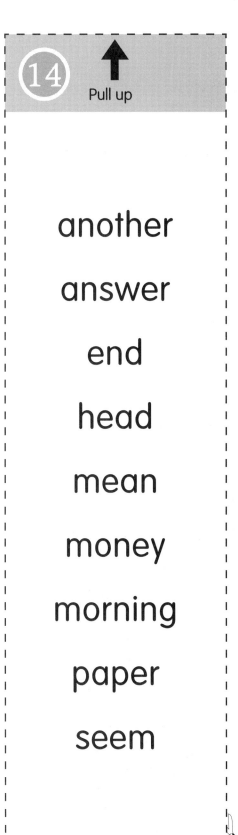

(14) ↑ Pull up

another

answer

end

head

mean

money

morning

paper

seem

EMC 3378 • © Evan-Moor Corp.

14

Ask and Answer

WOW!
I can read these words!

_____
Name

High-Frequency Words: Stories and Activities
EMC 3378 • © Evan-Moor Corp.

Ask and
Answer

 High-Frequency Words: Stories and Activities • EMC 3378 • © Evan-Moor Corp.

Learn New Words

Read each word out loud. Then write the missing letters.

also	even	large	more
al__ __	__ven	larg__	__ore
__ __so	e__ __ __	l__ __ge	m__ __e
a__ __o	e__e__	__ar__e	mor__

most	than	which
mos__	__ __an	whi__ __
mo__ __	th__n	__ __ich
__ost	tha__	wh__ch

Read each word. Then write the word on the lines.

1. than   ___ ___ ___ ___

2. more   ___ ___ ___ ___

3. even   ___ ___ ___ ___

4. large   ___ ___ ___ ___ ___

5. most   ___ ___ ___ ___

6. also   ___ ___ ___ ___

7. which   ___ ___ ___ ___ ___

Practice New Words

Read the first sentence in each box.
Then fill in the blanks with the underlined words.

1. <u>Most</u> of the girls said they like cats <u>more</u> than dogs.

   _____ boys than girls said they like dogs _____ of all.

2. Do you like the big car <u>more</u> <u>than</u> the little one?

   No, I like the little car _____ _____ the big one.

3. Do you like the <u>large</u> fish <u>also</u>?

   I _____ like the _____ fish.

4. I <u>even</u> like the <u>large</u> pig.

   Is the _____ pig a thing that _____ Mom would like?

5. I like fish <u>most</u> of all, but I <u>also</u> like eggs.

   Dad _____ likes fish, but he likes eggs the _____.

6. What does Don like <u>even</u> more <u>than</u> dogs?

   Don likes birds _____ more _____ dogs.

Read Naming Words

Read the words.

  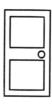

coat   coats   door   flower

Complete the sentences. Use the words above.

1. That _____ has many black seeds.

2. You can open the _____ to the large room.

3. I need my _____ because it is cold.

4. Will you also put the _____ in some water?

Circle the word that best completes each sentence.
Then read each sentence out loud.

1. My cat can sing, and she can even open a (**do**, **door**)!

2. I like the orange (**flower**, **follow**) more than the yellow one.

3. Which (**cold**, **coats**) do you like most?

4. That (**coat**, **coats**) is too large for me.

Read the story. Then color the coats so they look like the ones in the story.

Which Do You Like Most?

Mom and Hanna went in the door. They were in the store they liked best. Mom said, "We each need a coat. This place will have a large coat for me. It also will have a little coat for you."

After a while, Hanna asked, "Which coats do you like?"

Mom said, "I like this green coat more than the red one. I even like this black coat. But I like this blue coat most of all. I like the yellow apples on it. Which coats do you like?"

Hanna said, "I like this red coat. I also like this pink one. I like them even more than this blue coat. Most of all, I like this purple coat with the flower on it."

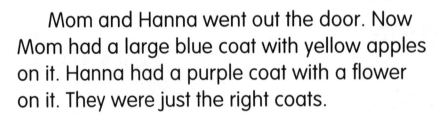

Mom and Hanna went out the door. Now Mom had a large blue coat with yellow apples on it. Hanna had a purple coat with a flower on it. They were just the right coats.

 High-Frequency Words: Stories and Activities • EMC 3378 •

Note: Follow the directions on page 5.

Get Ready, Get Set, Read!

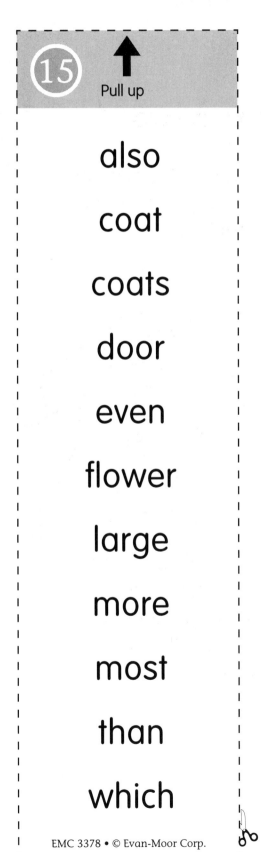

15 Pull up ↑

also

coat

coats

door

even

flower

large

more

most

than

which

EMC 3378 • © Evan-Moor Corp.

15

Which Do You Like Most?

_____

_____

WOW! I can read these words!

_____
Name

High-Frequency Words: Stories and Activities
EMC 3378 • © Evan-Moor Corp.

Which Do You Like Most?

Name _____

Color a star for every word you read. Write how many.

I Can Read!

☆ also
☆ another
☆ answer
☆ call
☆ color
☆ does
☆ end
☆ even
☆ fast
☆ father
☆ follow
☆ goes
☆ large
☆ learn
☆ mean
☆ more
☆ morning

I can read ____ words.

I Can Read!

☆ most
☆ never
☆ night
☆ off
☆ or
☆ school
☆ seem
☆ sing
☆ sleep
☆ spell
☆ study
☆ tell
☆ than
☆ use
☆ which
☆ year

I can read ____ words.

fold

YOU ARE A STAR!

I can read 100 sight words!

_____
Name

Answer Key

Page 10

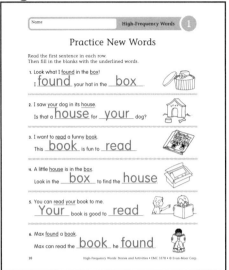

Page 11

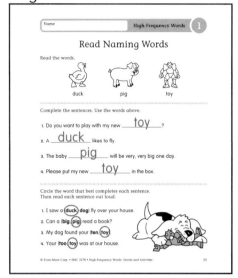

Page 16

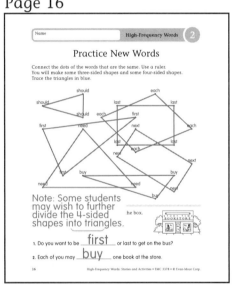

Page 17

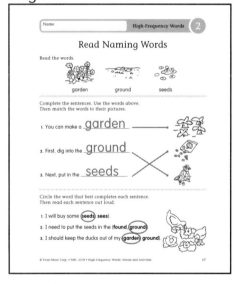

Page 22

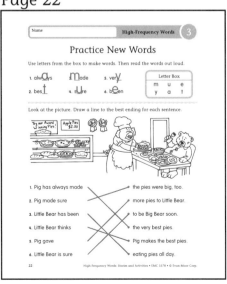

Page 23

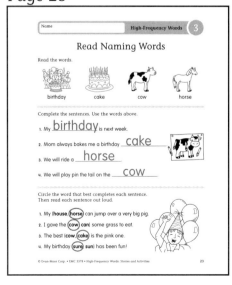

Page 28

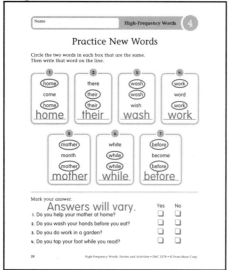

Page 29

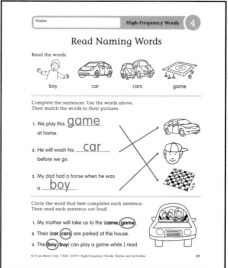

Page 34

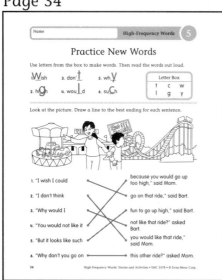

Page 35

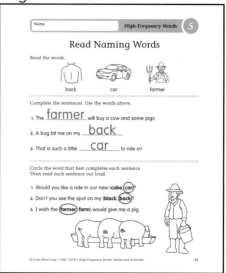

Page 42

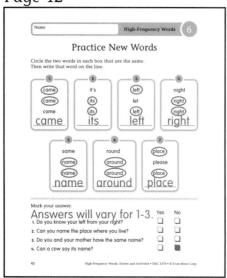

Page 43

High-Frequency Words—Stories and Activities • EMC 3378 • © Evan-Moor Corp.

Page 48

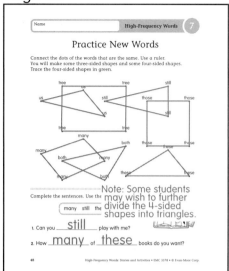

Page 49

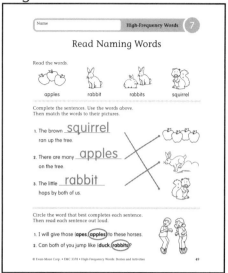

Page 54

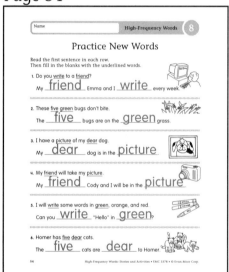

Page 55

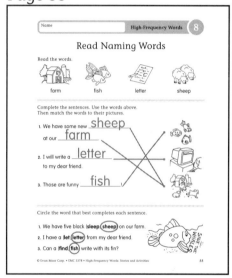

Page 60

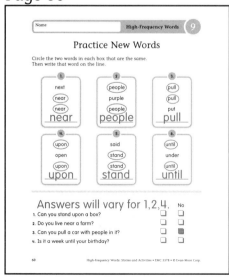

Page 61

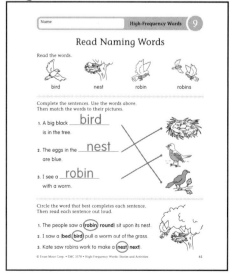

Page 66

Practice New Words

Read the first sentence in each row.
Then fill in the blanks with the underlined words.

1. You had a <u>different</u> <u>ball</u> last week.
   How was the ___ball___ ___different___?

2. I like to <u>sit</u> in a <u>cold</u> pool when it is hot.
   Is the pool too ___cold___ to ___sit___ in?

3. We must <u>move</u> this big <u>thing</u>.
   Where must you ___move___ this ___thing___?

4. Please <u>leave</u> the <u>ball</u> at home.
   I will ___leave___ the ___ball___ there.

5. I want to <u>move</u> to a <u>different</u> house.
   What is ___different___ about this ___move___?

6. Where should I <u>sit</u> when you <u>leave</u>?
   When I ___leave___ you can ___sit___ here.

66   High-Frequency Words: Stories and Activities • EMC 3378 • © Evan-Moor Corp.

Page 67

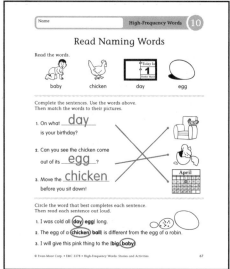

Read Naming Words

Read the words.

baby   chicken   day   egg

Complete the sentences. Use the words above.
Then match the words to their pictures.

1. On what ___day___ is your birthday?

2. Can you see the chicken come out of its ___egg___?

3. Move the ___chicken___ before you sit down!

Circle the word that best completes each sentence.
Then read each sentence out loud.

1. I was cold all (day) egg) long.
2. The egg of a (chicken) ball) is different from the egg of a robin.
3. I will give this pink thing to the (big (baby)).

© Evan-Moor Corp. • EMC 3378 • High-Frequency Words: Stories and Activities   67

Page 74

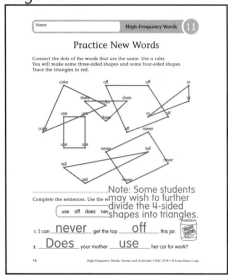

Practice New Words

Connect the dots of the words that are the same. Use a ruler.
You will make some three-sided shapes and some four-sided shapes.
Trace the triangles in red.

color   off   off   or
    does   does
color   off   off
    use   does
        off   never
use   use
    never   tell
tell
    never   tell
tell   never

Note: Some students may wish to further divide the 4-sided shapes into triangles.

Complete the sentences. Use the w...

use   off   does   nev...

1. I can ___never___ get the top ___off___ this jar.

2. ___Does___ your mother ___use___ her car for work?

74   High-Frequency Words: Stories and Activities • EMC 3378 • © Evan-Moor Corp.

Page 75

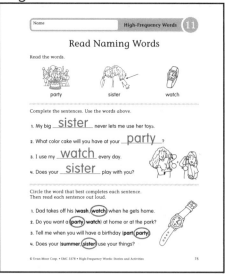

Read Naming Words

Read the words.

party   sister   watch

Complete the sentences. Use the words above.

1. My big ___sister___ never lets me use her toys.

2. What color cake will you have at your ___party___?

3. I use my ___watch___ every day.

4. Does your ___sister___ play with you?

Circle the word that best completes each sentence.
Then read each sentence out loud.

1. Dad takes off his (wash (watch)) when he gets home.
2. Do you want a (party) watch) at home or at the park?
3. Tell me when you will have a birthday (part (party)).
4. Does your (summer (sister)) use your things?

© Evan-Moor Corp. • EMC 3378 • High-Frequency Words: Stories and Activities   75

Page 80

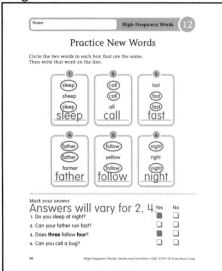

Practice New Words

Circle the two words in each box that are the same.
Then write that word on the line.

1. sleep / sheep / sleep → ___sleep___
2. call / call / all → ___call___
3. last / fast / fast → ___fast___
4. father / father / farmer → ___father___
5. follow / yellow / follow → ___follow___
6. night / right / night → ___night___

Mark your answer.

Answers will vary for 2, 4   Yes   No

1. Do you sleep at night?   ☐   ☐
2. Can your father run fast?   ☐   ☐
3. Does three follow four?   ☐   ☐
4. Can you call a bug?   ☐   ☐

80   High-Frequency Words: Stories and Activities • EMC 3378 • © Evan-Moor Corp.

Page 81

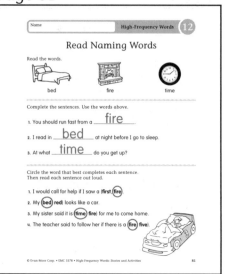

Read Naming Words

Read the words.

bed   fire   time

Complete the sentences. Use the words above.

1. You should run fast from a ___fire___
2. I read in ___bed___ at night before I go to sleep.
3. At what ___time___ do you get up?

Circle the word that best completes each sentence.
Then read each sentence out loud.

1. I would call for help if I saw a (first (fire)).
2. My (bed) red) looks like a car.
3. My sister said it is (time) fire) for me to come home.
4. The teacher said to follow her if there is a (fire) five).

© Evan-Moor Corp. • EMC 3378 • High-Frequency Words: Stories and Activities   81

Page 86

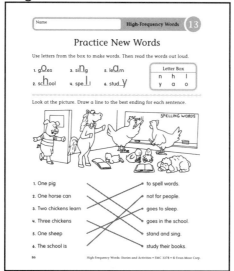

Practice New Words

Use letters from the box to make words. Then read the words out loud.

1. g O es   3. si n g   5. le a rn

2. sc h ool   4. spe l l   6. stud y

Letter Box
n h l
y a o

Look at the picture. Draw a line to the best ending for each sentence.

1. One pig — goes to sleep.
2. One horse can — stand and sing.
3. Two chickens learn — goes in the school.
4. Three chickens — to spell words.
5. One sheep — not for people.
6. The school is — study their books.

86   High-Frequency Words: Stories and Activities • EMC 3378 • © Evan-Moor Corp.

Page 87

Read Naming Words

Read the words.

boy   children   song

Complete the sentences. Use the words above.

1. We will learn to sing a __song__ this year.
2. The __children__ study their books.
3. That __boy__ goes to my school.
4. Can the __children__ spell all the words?

Circle the word that best completes each sentence. Then read each sentence out loud.

1. Did that (song, **boy**) go to our school last year?
2. The (child, **children**) learn to spell words every day.
3. Would you like to sing a (**song**, spring)?
4. One of their children is a (**boy**, bug).

© Evan-Moor Corp. • EMC 3378 • High-Frequency Words: Stories and Activities   87

Page 92

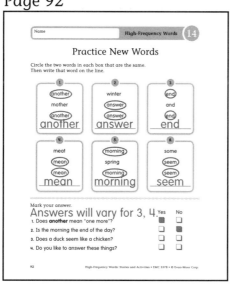

Practice New Words

Circle the two words in each box that are the same. Then write that word on the line.

1. another / mother / another → __another__
2. winter / answer / answer → __answer__
3. end / and / end → __end__
4. meat / mean / mean → __mean__
5. morning / spring / morning → __morning__
6. some / seem / seem → __seem__

Mark your answer.
Answers will vary for 3, 4.

         Yes   No
1. Does **another** mean "one more"? ■ □
2. Is the morning the end of the day? □ ■
3. Does a duck seem like a chicken? □ □
4. Do you like to answer these things? □ □

92   High-Frequency Words: Stories and Activities • EMC 3378 • © Evan-Moor Corp.

Page 93

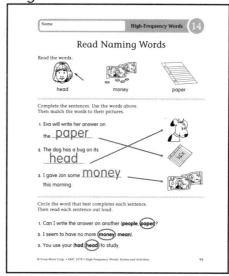

Read Naming Words

Read the words.

head   money   paper

Complete the sentences. Use the words above. Then match the words to their pictures.

1. Eva will write her answer on the __paper__
2. The dog has a bug on its __head__
3. I gave Jon some __money__ this morning.

Circle the word that best completes each sentence. Then read each sentence out loud.

1. Can I write the answer on another (people, **paper**)?
2. I seem to have no more (**money**, mean).
3. You use your (had, **head**) to study.

© Evan-Moor Corp. • EMC 3378 • High-Frequency Words: Stories and Activities   93

Page 98

Practice New Words

Read the first sentence in each box. Then fill in the blanks with the underlined words.

1. Most of the girls said they like cats more than dogs.
__More__ boys than girls said they like dogs __most__ of all.

2. Do you like the big car more than the little one?
No, I like the little car __more than__ the big one.

3. Do you like the large fish also?
I __also__ like the __large__ fish.

4. I even like the large pig.
Is the __large__ pig a thing that __even__ Mom would like?

5. I like fish most of all, but I also like eggs.
Dad __also__ likes fish, but he likes eggs the __most__.

6. What does Don like even more than dogs?
Don likes birds __even__ more __than__ dogs.

98   High-Frequency Words: Stories and Activities • EMC 3378 • © Evan-Moor Corp.

Page 99

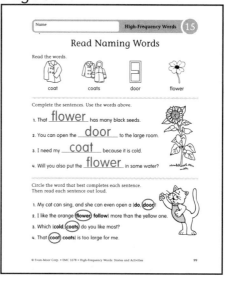

Read Naming Words

Read the words.

coat   coats   door   flower

Complete the sentences. Use the words above.

1. That __flower__ has many black seeds.
2. You can open the __door__ to the large room.
3. I need my __coat__ because it is cold.
4. Will you also put the __flower__ in some water?

Circle the word that best completes each sentence. Then read each sentence out loud.

1. My cat can sing, and she can even open a (do, **door**)!
2. I like the orange (**flower**, follow) more than the yellow one.
3. Which (cold, **coats**) do you like most?
4. That (**coat**, coats) is too large for me.

© Evan-Moor Corp. • EMC 3378 • High-Frequency Words: Stories and Activities   99

Evan-Moor's Read and Understand

The **Read and Understand** series provides teachers with a comprehensive resource of stories and skills pages to supplement any core reading program. Use as directed lessons or independent practice.

Read and Understand Stories and Activities

Resource books containing reproducible stories and practice materials for a wide spectrum of reading skills. More than 20 stories included, with fun illustrations. An answer key is provided. 144 pages. **Correlated to state standards.**

Grade K	EMC 637	**Grade 3**	EMC 640
Grade 1	EMC 638	**Grades 4–6+, Fiction**	EMC 748
Grade 2	EMC 639	**Grades 4–6+, Nonfiction**	EMC 749

More Read and Understand Stories and Activities

Provides teachers with a comprehensive resource of stories and skills pages to supplement any core reading program. The practice activities following each story include a comprehension page, a vocabulary page, and a phonics or structural analysis page. 144 pages. **Correlated to state standards.**

Grade 1	EMC 745
Grade 2	EMC 746
Grade 3	EMC 747